Western Europe

Jennifer Prior, Ph.D.

Consultants

William O'Mara, Ph.D.
History Professor
California State University, Dominguez Hills

Jon Anger
English, History, and ELD Teacher
Novato Unified School District

Publishing Credits

Rachelle Cracchiolo, M.S.Ed., *Publisher*
Emily R. Smith, M.A.Ed., *SVP of Content Development*
Véronique Bos, *Vice President of Creative*
Dani Neiley, *Editor*
Fabiola Sepulveda, *Series Graphic Designer*

Image Credits: p.9 (top) Shutterstock/WH_Pics; p.9 (bottom) Shutterstock/Trabantos; p.11 (top) Shutterstock/Everett Collection; p.13 (bottom) Shutterstock/Nataliya Hora; p.14 (top) Shutterstock/FooTToo; p.16 (bottom) Shutterstock/Jasper Image; p.17 (top) Shutterstock/4kclips; p.20 (top) Shutterstock/Lunopark; p.21 (top) Getty Images/ Jane Barlow–PA Images; p.21 (bottom) Shutterstock/Marco Ciccolella; p.22 (bottom) Shutterstock/Sorbis; p.23 (bottom) Shutterstock/Barry Barnes; p.24 Alamy/Reuters; p.25 (bottom) Shutterstock/Cristiano Barni; all other images from iStock and/or Shutterstock

Library of Congress Cataloging-in-Publication Data

Names: Prior, Jennifer Overend, 1963- author.
Title: Western Europe / Jennifer Prior.
Description: Huntington Beach, CA : Teacher Created Materials, Inc, [2023]
| Includes index. | Audience: Ages 8-18 | Summary: "The region of
western Europe has a range of cultures. The land varies from rocky
coasts to rolling hills. It has sandy beaches and impressive mountain
ranges. Its history has, at times, been turbulent. Today, it is a
thriving region both financially and politically. It is known for great
food and world-famous art. And discoveries made by its people have
affected the world"-- Provided by publisher.
Identifiers: LCCN 2022038218 (print) | LCCN 2022038219 (ebook) | ISBN
9781087695129 (paperback) | ISBN 9781087695280 (ebook)
Subjects: LCSH: Europe, Western--Juvenile literature
Classification: LCC D967 .P75 2023 (print) | LCC D967 (ebook) | DDC
940--dc23/eng/20220817
LC record available at https://lccn.loc.gov/2022038218
LC ebook record available at https://lccn.loc.gov/2022038219

Shown on the cover is Amsterdam,
Netherlands.

5482 Argosy Avenue
Huntington Beach, CA 92649
www.tcmpub.com
ISBN 978-1-0876-9512-9

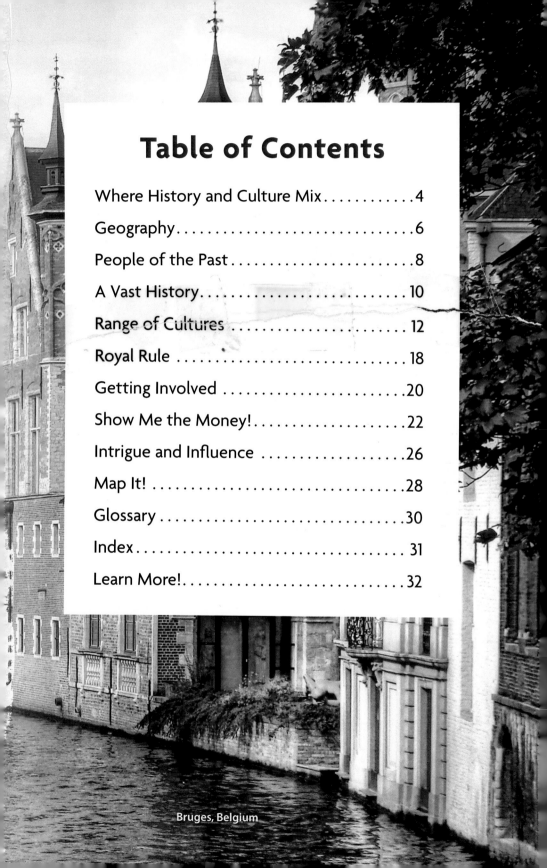

Table of Contents

Bruges, Belgium

Where History and Culture Mix

Of the world's seven continents, Europe is the second smallest. But it has the third largest number of people. It consists of 44 countries. It is surrounded on three sides by water, and part of it is made up of islands. The United Nations divides Europe into four regions: western, eastern, northern, and southern. This book focuses on western Europe.

When thinking of western Europe, most people think of great landmarks. There's the Eiffel Tower in France. And, Big Ben is in London. But there is more to know about the places and people in this part of the world. Western Europe is a mix of histories and cultures. It is a mix of languages and landscapes. It has both mild and cold climates. Each country has a **unique** culture. And the world depends on these countries for their many contributions.

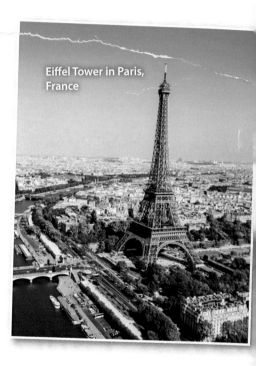

Eiffel Tower in Paris, France

Oeschinen Lake in Switzerland

ELAND

FAROE ISLANDS
(Denmark)

Norwegian
Sea

NORWAY

Gulf of
Bothnia

SWEDEN

SCOTLAND

NORTHERN IRELAND

North Sea

DENMARK

Baltic Sea

RUSSIA

IRELAND

ISLE
OF MAN

WALES   ENGLAND

NETHERLANDS

POLAND

GERMANY

Celtic Sea

English Channel

BELGIUM

CHANNEL ISLANDS

LUXEMBOURG

CZECHIA

SLOVAKIA

LIECHTENSTEIN

AUSTRIA

HUNGARY

SWITZERLAND

SLOVENIA

FRANCE

CROATIA

SAN
MARINO

BOSNIA &
HERZEGOVINA

SERBIA

Bay of Biscay

KOSOVO

MONACO

ITALY

Adriatic
Sea

MONTENEGRO

NORTH
MACEDONIA

ANDORRA

VATICAN
CITY

ALBANIA

PORTUGAL

SPAIN

GREECE

GIBRALTAR

MALTA

Mediterranean Sea

MOROCCO

ALGERIA

TUNISIA

LIBYA

Geography

Some countries in western Europe are **landlocked**. This includes Luxembourg, Switzerland, and Austria. Other countries border bodies of water. Germany, Belgium, and the Netherlands border the North Sea. France borders the Atlantic in the north. It borders the Mediterranean Sea in the south. Monaco, Italy, and Spain also rest along the Mediterranean. There are several islands in this region. The United Kingdom and Ireland are islands in the Atlantic Ocean. Several countries are part of peninsulas. This includes Portugal and Spain. It also includes Sweden and Norway.

Mountain Ranges

There are two major mountain ranges in the region. The Pyrenees divide France and Spain. The Alps are much longer. The Alps run through several countries, including France, Germany, Austria, and Switzerland. People from all over the world flock to the Alps for tourism and outdoor fun. Both ranges get lots of snow in the winter.

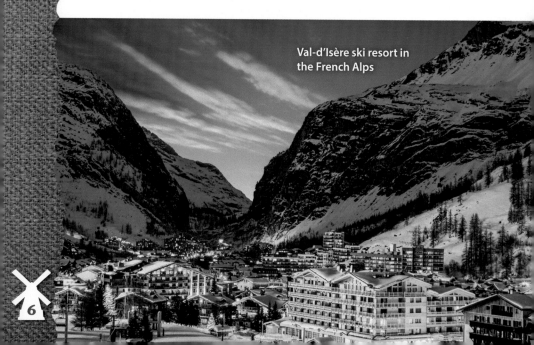

Val-d'Isère ski resort in the French Alps

Climate

Most of the region has a mild climate. This is caused by warm winds called *westerlies*. These winds pass over the warm ocean in the Caribbean. The wind stays warm as the Atlantic current carries it to Europe. Some areas, such as southern France and Italy, are warm and dry with mild winters. The farther north you go, the colder it gets in the winter. Winters can be very cold and snowy in Scotland, Norway, and Sweden, for example.

European Division, 1945–1991

Iron Curtain

Brrrr!

The Cold War began after World War II. War was never officially declared. But there was great tension between the United States and the Soviet Union. The Cold War affected all the countries in Europe. It led to the division of Europe into East and West by the invisible Iron Curtain. Most of these divisions dissolved at the end of the Cold War in 1991.

People of the Past

Indigenous peoples in western Europe have been traced back to prehistoric times.

Ancient Britain

In England, historians have found ancient stone tools buried across the land. These tools date back to one million years ago! This proves that the land has been **inhabited** for a long time. Agriculture was first introduced to the area around 4000 BCE. Immigrants brought this practice to the area. Farming was common in the southern part of the country. Historians have found evidence of huts shaped like circles and small fields. People who lived during this time used materials they could find on the land to make what they needed.

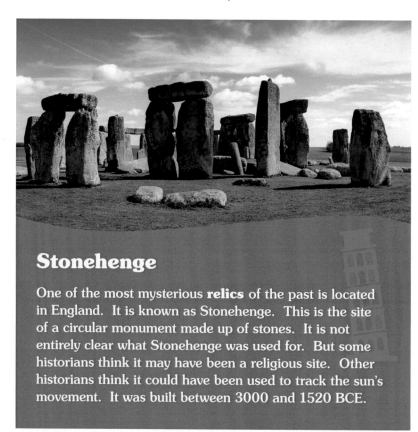

Stonehenge

One of the most mysterious **relics** of the past is located in England. It is known as Stonehenge. This is the site of a circular monument made up of stones. It is not entirely clear what Stonehenge was used for. But some historians think it may have been a religious site. Other historians think it could have been used to track the sun's movement. It was built between 3000 and 1520 BCE.

Iberian People

The Iberian people lived in what is now Spain and Portugal. They had complex forms of government. In the east, there were city-states. In the south, there were monarchies. They had their own system of writing, too. It was known as Iberian script. They used their writing system until the Romans took over their land. Then, they started using the Latin alphabet.

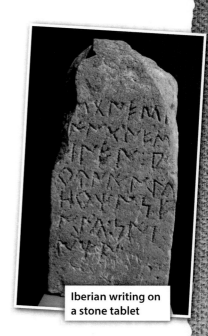

Iberian writing on a stone tablet

The Middle Ages

The period after the Roman Empire collapsed is known as the Middle Ages. This period lasted from 500 to 1500 CE. During this time, religion was very important. Christianity spread throughout Europe. Christianity was usually spread by force, and there were many wars because of it.

In the late 700s, **Vikings** were active. They made their homes in Norway, Sweden, and Denmark. They were farmers. And they also had remarkable sailing skills. They sailed their ships to many places in Europe. They were also warriors. In England, Scotland, and Ireland, they raided villages and tried to conquer land. They reached Iceland, and they even sailed to North America.

a Viking ship at a museum in Oslo, Norway

A Vast History

Western Europe's vast history spans centuries. Its society has been known for its **appreciation** of learning, exploration, and art. In the past 500 years, a lot has changed. European explorers traveled to land beyond Europe. The Reformation started in Germany and spread to other countries. It brought fierce conflicts about religion. Then, the Age of Enlightenment came. This era brought great new ideas by scientists. The following are some other notable periods.

The Industrial Revolution

This era began in England in the 1700s. It quickly spread all over Europe. And it spread to the United States. Before this time, many products were made by hand or simple machines. But the onset of steam-powered machines made mass production possible. These machines had more power, so goods could be made more quickly. Economies had once been based on farming. **Manufacturing** became more important instead.

cotton thread machines in a factory

An American plane drops a bomb on Germany in 1944.

World War II

The countries in western Europe were hit hard by World War II. In 1939, Germany invaded Poland. So, France and Britain declared war against the Germans. The Soviet Union and the United States joined in the conflict, too. Several smaller countries joined the **Allies** in the fight. These included Belgium and the Netherlands. The war lasted six years. It took a great **toll** on most countries in Europe.

European Union

In the 1990s, the European Union (EU) was formed. It is made of individual countries. It exists to provide security and peace. By 1995, there were 15 members of the EU. By 2020, there were 28 members. The United Kingdom broke away from the EU in 2020.

EU Countries

Range of Cultures

While the cultures of western Europe have blended over time, each country is unique. Let's explore a handful of them.

Austria

Austria's culture is influenced by Germany and Switzerland. Many classical composers are from Austria, including Wolfgang Mozart. The arts and literature are popular here. You can visit the opera or countless museums in Vienna. Winter sports are common here because of the Alps.

Vienna State Opera in Vienna, Austria

Belgium

Belgium is a diverse place with people from many cultures. It is characterized by close families and communities that support one another. Chocolate is one of Belgium's top exports. Many famous chocolatiers can be found here. These people make and sell chocolate. Belgium is also the home of the Smurfs cartoon.

a chocolate shop in Brussels, Belgium

Official Languages

In Portugal, the official language is Portuguese. Spain's official language is Spanish. These languages sound different from each other. But when you compare certain words, there are similarities. If you are fluent in Spanish, you may have an easier time learning how to read Portuguese!

English:
heart

Spanish:
corazón

Portuguese:
coração

England

Traditional English culture has influenced much of the world. Famous scientists, such as Sir Isaac Newton and Charles Darwin, were from England. Traditional English food includes bangers and mash, fish and chips, and bubble and squeak. Bubble and squeak is leftover vegetables, such as potatoes and brussels sprouts, fried together.

bangers and mash

France

France is known for its food, fashion, and art. Sharing long meals with friends and family is a common practice in France. No trip to Paris, France, is complete without a visit to the Louvre. It is the largest museum in the world. Some of the most famous paintings in the world are in the Louvre, including Leonardo da Vinci's *Mona Lisa*. Claude Monet and Edgar Degas are other famous French artists.

the Louvre

Germany

Germans value their families and neighbors. Oktoberfest (with great food and drink) is an annual tradition in the state of Bavaria. German culture is also known for its folk music. Some of the world's great composers, including Johann Sebastian Bach, were from Germany.

Oktoberfest celebration in Munich, Germany

Ireland

St. Patrick's day is a well-known holiday, but there is much more to Irish culture. People in Ireland love both modern and folk music. Each year, they promote Irish folk music with a festival that is popular throughout the country. And if you eat Irish **cuisine**, there are bound to be potatoes on your plate.

Harps are commonly used in Irish folk music.

Italian Food

Many foods besides pasta and pizza are popular in Italy. People along the coastlines often enjoy seafood. People eat lots of meat in central Italy, including wild boar. Polenta comes from Italy. It is a dish made of boiled cornmeal. Gelato also comes from Italy. It is a frozen dessert that is usually richer and thicker than ice cream.

gelato

Luxembourg

pork collar with broad beans and potatoes

The culture of Luxembourg is heavily influenced by the cultures of France, Germany, and Belgium. The national dish is pork collar with broad beans. But another unique food item is black pudding. In Luxembourg, this dish is made from animal blood. It is mixed with fat and vegetables, such as cabbage and onion. Then, it is formed into sausage. It is a popular breakfast item.

Monaco

Monaco is a very small country on the coast of France. Most people there are quite rich. In fact, one in every three people is a millionaire! The Grimaldi family rules the nation. In addition to running the country, the family has many **foundations**. These support the arts. The foundations also support initiatives that care for the environment. One initiative works toward ocean conservation.

Monte-Carlo, Monaco

Netherlands

Dutch people live in the Netherlands. When people think of Dutch society, they typically think of wooden shoes or windmills. But there is more to their culture. Dutch people appreciate and support the arts. Famous painters Rembrandt van Rijn and Vincent van Gogh were Dutch. And there are many art museums in the country.

tulips and windmills in the Netherlands

The country's wide beaches are popular for outdoor activities. People love to ride bikes, go ice skating, and play field hockey.

Scotland

Hundreds of years ago, Scots lived in small groups or clans. Today, they remember their past by participating in games, music, and dance. The Scottish Highland Games are a popular event today. The games include bagpipe music and athletic competitions. People at the Highland Games may wear traditional clothing. Men will often wear kilts. These are like knee-length skirts made of tartan fabric. A kilt represents a clan.

bagpipe players at the Highland Games in Scotland

Switzerland

Switzerland's culture is very diverse. It includes elements of the countries that surround it. This can be seen in Switzerland's four official languages. They are German, French, Italian, and Romansh.

In rural areas of Switzerland, some old traditions are still practiced. This includes yodeling, which is a type of singing. It also includes playing the alphorn. This is a very long horn with an end that rests on the ground.

Wales

In Wales, people love the arts and are known for their all-male choirs. They are **passionate** about their **rugby** teams. And many famous authors are from Wales. This includes Dylan Thomas, a famous poet. More than 29 percent of people in Wales speak Welsh. They have preserved this language for more than 1,000 years.

National Parks

Western Europe is home to some stunning national parks. One park in Norway has the European mainland's largest glacier. Norway's oldest national park is known as Rondane. If you visit, you might see some wild reindeer!

reindeer

Rondane National Park, Norway

Royal Rule

A monarchy is a form of government. Typically, that means a king or queen is in charge. The king or queen is part of a royal family. In the past, much of Europe was ruled by monarchs.

Spanish royal family

The governments in the United Kingdom and Belgium are called *constitutional monarchies*. This is true for the Netherlands, Luxembourg, Sweden, Norway, and Spain, too. That means the royal families do not make political decisions. Those who are elected by the people engage in politics. Royal families, instead, offer an identity to a nation. They bring the people together.

Take It to a Vote

Italy's government used to be a monarchy. But after World War II, the Italians voted. They changed their government to a democratic republic. They created a constitution and established legislative, executive, and judicial branches. Today, the head of the government is a prime minister.

Monaco is a monarchy that also has elected officials. The prince has far more control than in some other monarchies. He is called *chief of state*. He works with the National Council. And they collaborate to make decisions.

France, Germany, and Ireland were once ruled by royal families. But that is not the case today. The people of France elect a president. The president then works with others to run the country. Ireland, Germany, and Denmark are parliamentary **democracies**. They each have a prime minister who works closely with a group of lawmakers. In Ireland, the person is called the *taoiseach* (TEE-shuhk). In Germany, the leader is called the *chancellor*. With their councils, these leaders pass laws and make decisions.

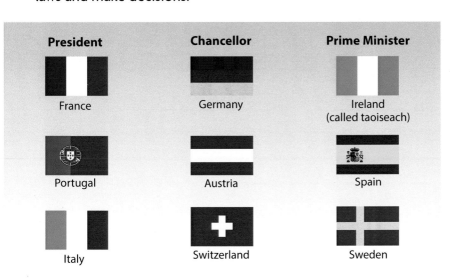

President	Chancellor	Prime Minister
France	Germany	Ireland (called taoiseach)
Portugal	Austria	Spain
Italy	Switzerland	Sweden

Getting Involved

Civic participation is about people getting involved to help their communities. This is valued throughout the western European region.

In Luxembourg, people are encouraged to vote. They are also encouraged to share thoughts about issues. For example, they discuss development of public spaces and how to address climate change.

People in Belgium get involved in many ways. They feed the hungry. They raise money for cancer research. They also work to care for the environment.

In the Netherlands, people care about their neighborhoods. They want to help improve them. They do volunteer work. They pick up trash to keep the landscape beautiful. Many also participate by voicing opinions. They give ideas about how money should be spent to help their communities.

People volunteer to pick up trash in Rotterdam, Netherlands.

Votes are counted for an election in Glasgow, Scotland.

Germans value civic education. They want their youth to grow up with a desire to get involved. They work to promote democracy. And they encourage children to learn about their roles in affecting politics.

The government and many groups in Scotland care about getting people involved. They have even created plans for how to do this. They want to hear from diverse groups. They also strive to build trust between the people and their leaders.

Raising Awareness

Greta Thunberg is a young activist from Sweden. She started a movement in 2018 called Fridays for Future. She went on a strike against climate change. Her actions caused ripples around the world. Young people began to protest, too. They protested in person and online. Today, Thunberg continues to raise awareness for climate change.

Show Me the Money!

Throughout much of Europe's history, **currency** was unique to each country. Imagine using one kind of money in Germany. You then cross the border into France and have to use a different kind of money. This can cause problems for people. First, not all money has the same value. The **exchange rate** changes all the time. Exchange rates go up and down depending on interest rates and inflation.

After the EU was formed, most of the EU countries adopted the same form of currency. It is called the *euro*. This made things much easier for people.

euro bills and coins

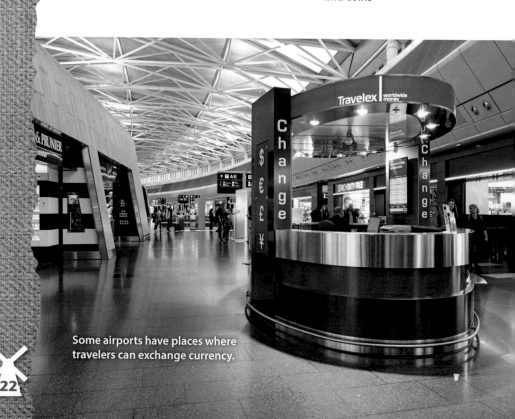

Some airports have places where travelers can exchange currency.

British pound notes

One exception was the United Kingdom (UK). The UK includes England, Wales, Northern Ireland, and Scotland. The UK was part of the EU for a while. But all four of its countries continued to use money called the *pound*. Denmark is another exception. Denmark uses money called the *krone*.

Money is not the only thing that the EU helps with. The EU also plays a role in trade for these countries. The EU works to make trade agreements. These can allow countries to import and export goods with one another.

Cash or Card?

It seems that much of the world operates without cash. Almost everywhere you go, a credit card can be used. But in Europe, it is important to have both on hand. Some restaurants only take cash. Some gas stations only take credit cards. So, it's best to be prepared and have both.

CARD AND CONTACTLESS PAYMENTS ONLY

We are currently not accepting cash

Thank you for your understanding

car factory in Cologne, Germany

Earning Money

Western Europe provides a vast number of products and services for the world. Most of the countries focused on farming in previous decades. But now, industries vary.

The UK and France produce **nuclear reactors**. The UK also makes military equipment. Manufacturing is a big industry in Wales. Forestry and fishing are industries in Wales, too. Scotland is known for **biotechnology**. It is also known for banking services.

Germany is a major supplier of **electronics**. It is also one of the largest car manufacturers.

Biotechnology

Biotechnology is a field that is far-reaching. It involves reducing diseases and saving lives. It also involves using different fuel sources. These are better for the planet. Biotechnology focuses on growing food more effectively.

The Netherlands is known for farming. In particular, the country produces dairy products. It is known for making butter, milk, and cheese. Hothouse tomatoes and other crops are grown in heated glass buildings there. And

greenhouses in the Netherlands

in more recent years, people in the Netherlands have focused on different areas of technology. It is very involved in the banking industry.

Luxembourg may be a small country, but it is big in the banking world. Banking services in this country are well-known around the globe.

Gambling is a large industry in Monaco. It is a prime spot for tourism. One popular event is the Monaco Grand Prix. This is a race car event that is held every year. People come from all over the world to watch.

Monaco Grand Prix

Intrigue and Influence

The many countries in western Europe draw people from all over the world. Whether it's vast expanses of tulips in the Netherlands, the French Riviera on the coast of France, or castle ruins in Scotland, there is much to see and do. Tourists come to see amazing landmarks. They visit historic buildings and see famous architecture. They enjoy world-famous art. They learn about great discoveries made by European citizens. The traditions, art, and cuisine are unique to each country.

After recovering from wars in the past, western Europe has come together into a thriving region. The many cultures of this region have blended in some ways. But they have all preserved their traditions and **distinct** histories.

Neuschwanstein Castle, Germany

The people of this region care about their communities. And they want to get involved. They help one another and make a difference in their communities. These countries provide a **wealth** of products and services to the world. Some of these products include raw materials, such as steel and lumber. Other products are grown or made. With all it has to offer, this prosperous region has a great influence on the world.

Let's Talk!

There are 24 official languages of the European Union. English is the most common. But French and German are identified as procedural languages, too. That means that business is done in all three languages. Most people in the region speak more than one language. Some even speak three or four!

Half Pipes   Fun Park

Benützung nur nach vorheriger Besichtigung

Utilisation uniquement après reconnaissance

Ispezionare l`impianto prima di utilizzario

Please inspect the site before using it

information board in the Alps

Villefranche-sur-Mer, French Riviera

Map It!

There are many cultures in western Europe. Each country is home to many groups of people. Create a map to show some of the key cultural activities, festivals, or traditions in a few countries.

1. Choose two countries, and create a map of them. Label their names and their capitals.

2. Research online to find information about the various cultures in these countries. Find out about their cultural activities.

3. Draw pictures or icons on your map to show what activities, festivals, or traditions are valued in different cultures.

4. Create a map key for the icons on your map. Each item in the map key should tell what the icon on the map means.

5. Share your map with a partner. Did you find different activities?

Oslo, Norway

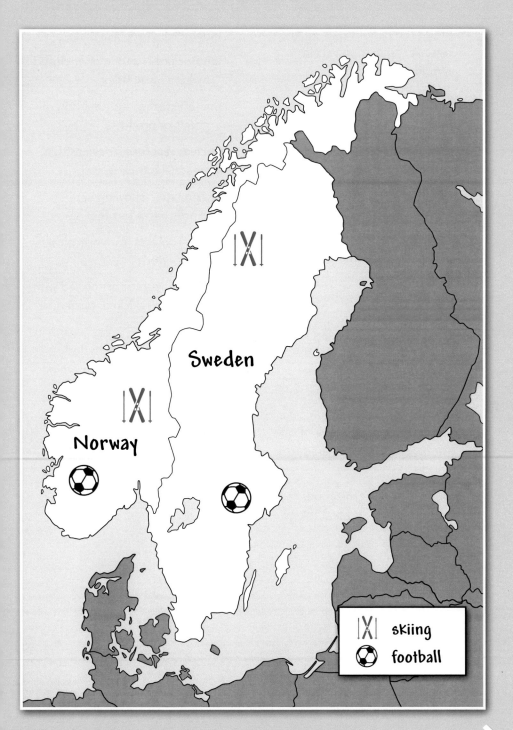

Norway

Sweden

skiing
football

Glossary

Allies—the nations that fought against the Axis powers in World War II

appreciation—a feeling of admiration

biotechnology—the manipulation of living cells to make new and useful products

cuisine—style of cooking

currency—money

democracies—forms of government in which people choose leaders by voting

distinct—not like others

electronics—devices that use electronic circuits, such as vacuums, radios, televisions, or cell phones

exchange rate—the value of one form of money compared to another

foundations—organizations that use money to do good things

inhabited—lived in a place

landlocked—shut in or enclosed by land on all sides

manufacturing—production of goods or products

nuclear reactors—devices that create electrical power

passionate—showing or expressing strong feeling

relics—objects from historical time periods

rugby—a team sport played with a ball that is kicked, carried, or passed to a goal

toll—emotional or physical damage caused by something

unique—one of a kind

Vikings—warriors who traveled by sea from Scandinavia between the late 700s to the 1000s

wealth—the state of being rich

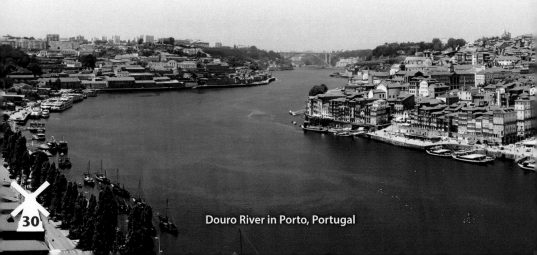

Douro River in Porto, Portugal

Index

Learn More!

Vincent van Gogh is a famous artist. He was from the Netherlands. He was very talented. But he had many struggles. Research to find answers to the following questions. Then, draw a paint palette on a sheet of paper. Write the answer to each question on a section of the palette.

- How did Van Gogh's parents feel about his career as an artist?

- What was unique about his art and use of color?

- What did he do to injure himself? Why did he do it?

- Find three more interesting facts about Van Gogh.

- Find the names of at least four of Van Gogh's paintings.

Wheat Field with Cypresses by Vincent van Gogh